extreme horticulture

john pfahl

extreme horticulture

john pfahl

introduction by
rebecca solnit

FRANCES LINCOLN

the botanical circus: adventures in american gardening

by rebecca solnit

Eden is the problem, of course. Eden stands as the idea of nature as it should be rather than as it is, and in attempting to make a garden resemble Eden the gardener wrestles it away from resembling nature – which is to say the uncultivated expanses around it, the patterns that would assert themselves without interference. If gardens were actual nature, we would just have a plot of land left alone outside, that wind and birds and proximate plants would seed and rain would water. Even in the humid temperate zones, let alone in America's desert southwest, a good deal of manipulation of soil and water is necessary to make something non-native grow. Eden serves as the phantasmagorical plan, the ideal nature, to which every gardener cleaves. But no two gardeners have quite the same vision of it, and some versions of paradise, as the pictures herein indicate, are very fabulous and unrestrained indeed. There are both individual variations and historical evolutions in the ideal of the garden as an improvement on nature, a paradise, and of course the word 'paradise' itself originally meant an enclosed garden, the kind of formal Islamic garden whose plans can be seen on most Persian carpets.

We love nature as a child loves a parent, but gardeners love their gardens as parents love children: with a preoccupied, hectoring, imposing love, not unlike that of museum curators, editors, animal tamers. Thoreau fretted over it in Walden, writing of the crop he grew with a gardener's contemplativeness:

I came to love my rows, my beans, though so many more than I wanted. They attached me to the earth, and so I got strength like Antaeus. But why should I raise them? Only heaven knows. This was my curious labor all summer – to make this portion of the earth's surface, which had yielded only cinquefoil, blackberries, johnswort, and the like, before, sweet wild fruits and pleasant flowers, produce instead this pulse. What shall I learn of beans or beans of me? I cherish them, I hoe them, early and late I have an eye to them; and this is my day's work. It is a fine broad leaf to look on. My auxiliaries are the dews and rains which water this dry soil. . . . My enemies are worms, cool days, and most of all woodchucks. . . . A long war, not with cranes, but with weeds, those Trojans who had sun and rain and dews on their side. Daily the beans saw me come to their rescue armed with a hoe, and thin the ranks of their enemies, filling up the trenches with weedy dead.[1]

Thoreau writes with such wryness because, as an American romantic, he admires the unaltered landscape, and that admiration itself is the fruit of a long European history of garden evolution and the control of nature. Nature was sufficiently abundant, even overwhelming, throughout most of human history that it didn't need to be referenced as an ideal, exactly. Some cultures assumed nature was fine as it was, making gardens unnecessary; others thought nature had fallen and yearned for an absent paradise whose parameters they sketched in herbs and flowers and walls, or in Asia with pines and pools and stones. Usually they yearned for a more visibly ordered nature. Our horticultural ancestors the Romans made topiary, espaliered trees and neatly patterned beds; their ideal nature partook of a geometry reminiscent of military formations. After them, one could say that gardens relaxed into boudoir-like sanctuaries for all the senses until safety, wealth and a returning preoccupation with geometrical order prompted the explosion of the formal garden in the seventeenth century. Gardens – aristocratic gardens, gardens of extraordinary expense – then reached a sort of Euclidean-Cartesian apogee in conical trees and long allées and managed fountains, and they spread into their surroundings as they grew larger and larger: Versailles, with its avenues to the horizon, is the ultimate example, a garden that poses a challenge to nature. A 1712 English guide describes part of an ideal garden's layout as having

two Squares, each having four Quarters, with Basons. It is terminated by a long Arbour, with three Cabinets facing the Walks and Pavilions. On the Right are Green-Plots cut, to answer the walks, having Water-works, as on the other Side. These are bounded by a double line of Cases and Yews, and behind, by green Niches for Seats and Figures. On the Side is a Parterre of Orange-Trees walled in, having Iron Grills against the Walks; and at the End is a Bason, with Cabinets and green Niches for Seats.[2]

Vintage postcard, Versailles, France. Coll. John Pfahl

The dictum that for every action there is an equal and opposite reaction is as true of gardening as it is of anything else: the English in the eighteenth century began to link formal gardens to despotism and generated a notion of idealized nature that is still with us. It was a tremendous reversal, full of its own contradictions.

The idea that unaltered nature might be as worthy of contemplation as gardens always had been was slipping into the collective imagination in that century, and nature – or rather Nature – became a goddess constantly invoked. A year after the garden manual cited above, Alexander Pope effused: 'There is certainly something in the amiable Simplicity of unadorned Nature, that spreads over the Mind a more noble sort of Tranquility, and a loftier Sensation of Pleasure, than can be raised from the nicer Scenes of Art.'[3] All the garden geometry of paths and parterres and, particularly, topiary had come to seem obnoxiously or at least ridiculously *unnatural*, that new term of condemnation, and Pope condemned the last with famous verve in an imaginary catalogue of topiaries: 'Adam and Eve in Yew; Adam a little shatter'd by the fall of the Tree of Knowledge in the Great Storm; Eve and the serpent very flourishing. St George in Box; his Arm scarce long enough, but will be in a Condition to stick the Dragon by next April. A green Dragon on the same, with a Tail of Ground-Ivy for the present. N.B. These two not to be Sold separately,' and so on.[4] The naturalistic garden known as the English garden evolved by degrees; parterres and topiary were done away with, and the gridded landscape gave way to serpentine paths and meanders, but sculpture and architecture still abounded until the middle of the century, when the inimitable 'Capability' Brown began to do away with them as well (and Humphrey Repton carried on Brown's grand scale and austere places, although he allowed back some of the ornamentation Brown had banished).

Of course, the English garden was imitating a very particular notion of nature, one that at least at first was found more in the paintings of Claude and Poussin and sometimes those of Salvator Rosa than in the surrounding countryside. So one of the great contradictions is that the English garden is imitating art in its attempt to imitate nature, and the nature it is willing to imitate is once again a very specific idealized thing, albeit a flowing, complex thing. The radical idea was that nature was already orderly (clearing the way to start questioning the Fall or even to go with Rousseau and see it as a fall from natural innocence into civilized corruption). One thing led to another, as plenty of garden histories recount at length, and the culmination of this naturalizing process was that the surrounding landscape was by the 1770s found worthy of contemplation and suitable for strolling, and scenic-appreciation guidebooks by the likes of William Gilpin replaced garden books as the manuals of appropriate aesthetic responsiveness. To some extent, the world ever since has been regarded as once only gardens were. It's a tremendous history, out of the garden and into the landscape, from where originated the outdoor industries and the environmental movement, perhaps even the idea of the national park. It's about a knight's move towards democracy – first towards gardens that, if they required less maintenance, required more space (a thousand-acre garden is only so democratic); but it opened the way to the view that the whole world was a garden, at which point one no longer needed privileged access: Hampstead Heath would do, or an excursion train, or a long walk away from the factory districts (the latter two so assiduously utilized into the mid-twentieth century in England, though nature never achieved that kind of populist status in America, perhaps because too many populists were still busy fleeing the farm). It recalls a parallel evolution in the visual arts in the second half of the twentieth century to

Humphrey Repton. From *Sketches and Hints on Landscape Gardening*, London, 1794. (Reproduced by permission of the Buffalo and Erie County Public Library, Buffalo, NY).

WASHINGTON MONUMENT AND CHERRY BLOSSOMS, WASHINGTON, D. C.

Vintage postcard, Washington D.C. Coll. John Pfahl

a position where, as Robert Irwin put it long before he himself became a garden designer, 'the object of art may be to eliminate the necessity of it.'[5]

The eighteenth-century dissolution of the garden into the landscape left only one unresolved question: what kinds of gardens were people going to have around their homes after that apotheoesis of Nature? Christopher Thacker writes: 'For several decades the nineteenth century had no distinctive garden style, but remained unsettled, eclectic and searching, as it did in architectural form, in furniture and in clothing.'[6] If the great eighteenth century impulse came out of the growing control men had over the world, a control that meant it was safe to let down the garden walls and satisfying to be occasionally overwhelmed by nature rather than to overwhelm it, then the nineteenth century saw very different impulses. Letting well enough alone was one of the few pastimes the Victorians never entertained. A new fussiness returned, as did the formalism of bright flowerbeds that no longer spoke of great Euclidean expanses of aristocratic order, just of the obsession with pattern and the bourgeois anxiety to sort it all out. And there was so much more to sort out. The Victorian garden comes perhaps from the botanic garden rather than the pleasure garden or landscape garden. And the botanic garden was less about the beauty of Eden itself than its symbolic and literal abundance. This is a shift in part from the garden as primarily a composition to the garden as a collection, and with that shift the garden regained its details – its flowers and unusual plants – lost in the rush towards naturalism. (For one of the peculiarities of garden history up until that point is how little it had been plant history. In landscape gardens, particularly, everything was meant to become a pleasing composition at a suitable distance; flowers were banished because such gardens were not about details and close-ups and individual phenomena, and they were certainly not about brightness.)

Early botanical gardens were sometimes divided into quarters, echoing both the paradise garden of the Islamic world (its central fountain and four streams echoing Eden's own hydrological arrangements) and the idea that the world's four continents were present as the four quarters of the garden. (Although the continents were eventually found out to be less symmetrical in number, other more practical versions of this order survive in, for example, Kew Gardens, with its greenhouses representing climates of varying degrees of intemperate pleasantness, or the Huntington Garden in California, with the continents reiterated as clusters amid the winding paths.) John Prest writes in his history of the botanic garden: 'It was as though the creation was a jigsaw puzzle. In the Garden of Eden, Adam and Eve had been introduced to the completed picture. When they sinned, God had put some of the pieces away in a cupboard – an American cupboard – to be released when mankind improved, or he saw fit.'[7] This is part of the reason why Thoreau was uncomfortable with 'making the earth say beans': America was already an Edenic garden in the rhetoric of his time, and he took to an extreme the idea of noninterference implicit in the English landscape garden. But the botanical garden was all about interference, eventually about the maximum interference of colonialism and conquest (these movements spread plants in all directions, so that apples and roses grew in the colonies while chrysanthemums and maize and monkey puzzle trees came to Europe). In the nineteenth century, plants poured in from around the world in increasing profusion, helped along by the growing availability of glass for greenhouses – making it possible to grow delicate and tropical plants in northern Europe – and by, in the 1830s, the invention of the Wardian case (of which no less an authority than Thacker says: 'The Wardian case is, with the ha-ha and the lawn-mower, one of the great inventions in garden history.'[8]) This was what we nowadays might call

Vintage postcard, Skagit Valley, Washington. Coll. John Pfahl

6309. GIANT CACTUS, PHOENIX, ARIZ.

Vintage postcard, Phoenix, Arizona. Coll. John Pfhal

a terrarium: a sealed glass box or bottle that made it possible to keep plants alive for the laborious months on shipboard back from Australia or Brazil.

There was a sort of golden age of plant hunters (echoed by the rainforest plant hunting now conducted by pharmaceutical companies and resisted as 'biocolonialism' by those forests' residents).[9] Orchids and other tropical flora were arriving in the West, and their status as trophies of conquest, as prizes of the hunt, were well recognized. Victorian gardeners seemed well aware of the status of these plants, and such gardens were didactic and imperial; small local places about colonies and continents and expeditions far away. It's hard to recapture the shock some plants must have produced. The American explorer John Wesley Powell on his first encounter with the flora of the southwestern deserts exclaimed in what sounds close to horror: 'The few plants are strangers to the dwellers in the temperate zone. On the mountains a few junipers and pinons are found, and cactuses, agave, and yuccas, low, fleshy plants with bayonets and thorns. The landscape of vegetal life is weird – no forests, no meadows, no green hills, no foliage, but clublike stems of plants armed with stilettos. Many of the plants bear gorgeous flowers.'[10] The jungle was equally alarming to the temperate-adjusted, with its dense, humid, three-dimensional landscape of vigorous life, vivid colour and perilous species. Only over time did these plants become part of the standard vocabulary, just as words like jodhpur and raccoon and canyon have. Almost no one thinks of Mexico when they look at dahlias (which the Aztecs called cocoxochitl). Marigolds and zinnias and rubber plants and bottlebrushes have become standard nursery offerings. Only through this history did we arrive at the present ahistorical anything-goes moment of gardens, in which topiary and exotics and wildernesses and abundance and Zen gardens and statuary all jostle each other. It is as though all the aesthetics, traditions and regions have collapsed into an enormous polyglot vocabulary, a vocabulary in which anything may be said. This is the moment in which Extreme Horticulture takes place, though the images here seem to reflect an American exuberance and lawlessness that too has a history.

The United States was already wildly excessive and uninhibited on two fronts when it came to making gardens. For one thing the landscape itself was of a spectacularly un-European scale in its individual features, its Niagara Falls and Grand Canyon and ten-mile-long bison herds and mile-wide Mississippi and sequoias more like skyscrapers than other trees, and in its overall vastness and variety of mountains, deserts, prairies, forests, wetlands and so forth. Secondly, within this expansive terrain, the European-Americans were living off largely introduced crops, though corn, squash, potatoes and chillies came from native agriculture, and life was already hybrid, jumbled, patchwork, with its native, its European and its share of the plants coming from the other parts of the world at that time. The terrains, the climates, the hybrid populations and plantings all encouraged an unorthodoxy that was harder to come by in the old countries; the American lack of a past always made the future seem more available, and more wide open.

The difference between Britain and America is the difference between Alice, daughter of a don, falling down a rabbit hole (a very expansive, peculiar rabbit hole, admittedly), and Dorothy, orphan raised by Kansas farmers, taken up by a tornado. Alice wanders a dreamland of decorous delirium, with its playing-card chattels, its small animals, rose gardens, tea parties, chessboards and nursery rhyme characters. The landscape of the Wizard of Oz, with the angry apple trees, the endless expanse of poppies, live scarecrows, talking lions, witches, midgets, Emerald City, tornados – the scale of pecularity, the available vocabulary of

strangeness, the volatility is that much more vast. (American excess is evident too in the way L. Frank Baum spun the story of Oz out into a series of more than a dozen books that other writers continued after his death, while Alice's history has its Old Testament in Wonderland and its New through the looking glass, and no more.) English gardens are sometimes Wonderland, but American gardens easily slip into Oz.

Thomas Brayton, for example, acquired a seven-acre parcel of land in New England in 1872 and began a topiary garden, but one whose scope would have dizzied even the sarcastic Alexander Pope. Though topiary was a strictly European tradition, Brayton's Green Animals garden is a global menagerie with a topiary giraffe, bear, swan, ostrich, hippopotamus, peacock (and a stray terrier, out of scale of course, though not as out of scale as Jeff Koons'). The peculiarity of the place is that it isn't aspiring to what the old topiary gardens did, a kind of gracious harmony that made its makers seem an estimable part of the place. It's a literal zoological gardens, an eclectic collection of images from all over the world. This is a far more reckless revolt against good taste than all the garden gnomes in Northumberland could organize, one that isn't merely kitschy, but heroically preposterous. In Brayton's time county fairs were at their apogee, and they exhibited not only exemplary but extreme examples of local agriculture. (Giant pumpkins particularly are a hallowed American tradition going strong today; the iconic American children's author Laura Ingalls Wilder tells a tale of her spouse in his youth exhibiting one at a New York county fair in about the 1850s,[11] and the comic strip *Peanuts* featured a Great Pumpkin deity for Hallowe'en akin to Santa and the Easter Bunny.) Brayton started out just as Buffalo Bill was becoming the performer whose theatrics would culminate in Buffalo Bill's Wild America, a sort of bioregional circus that toured North

Vintage 'Exaggerations' postcard, Dixon, Illinois. Coll. John Pfahl

America and Europe, and a couple of years after P. T. Barnum's efforts culminated in the founding of Barnum and Bailey's circus, still touring today.

Think of P. T. Barnum as a gardener for a moment. Gardeners seek to alter their plants and to push them to extremes, and Barnum sought out human beings who were similarly unusual. He began his career exhibiting an African-American woman who claimed to be the 161-year-old nurse of George Washington's father, soon acquired a mermaid skeleton, and was truly launched when he enlisted the services of young Charles Stratton, still remembered well as General Tom Thumb, a midget who eventually reached the height of 33 inches. Thus began the Golden Age of circuses and the American sideshow or, as it was known at Coney Island in New York, the freak show: a sort of botanical garden of human variety from around the world, often including Siamese twins (seldom Siamese but always so designated after Chang and Eng, two of Barnum's performers), giants, dwarfs, midgets, fat ladies, living skeletons, pinheads, hermaphrodites, strong men, bearded ladies, contortionists, sword-swallowers, fire-eaters, tattooed, limbless and otherwise unusual people. The botanical equivalent might be bonsai, sequoia, grafts, dwarf and espaliered fruit trees, barrel cacti, banyan trees, hybrid tea roses such as 'Racy Lady' and 'Scent Sation', tropical flowers bred to yet more extravagant displays, tulip breaks, and, of course, topiary and outsize pumpkins. (Just as in the sideshow most of the freaks need do nothing more than be their unusual selves, so sunflowers and azaleas and the largest fig tree in the United States may sit serene in their fabulousness, but topiary is performative flora, akin to sword-swallowers and acrobats in its achievement of an effect that is the result of effort, not essence: topiary is, after all, usually nothing more exotic than box or yew.)

Whole forests have been laid low for books on beauty and, in the eighteenth and early nineteenth centuries, the sublime and the picturesque. All of these aesthetics can be configured as being uplifting, enlarging, somehow in good taste. But there are other aesthetics, not least among them what could be called the exuberant, the peculiar, the disproportionate, the unusual and exotic, the outsized, the gaudy, the excessive, the appalling. The desire for beauty is considered to be uplifting, so long as it doesn't shade over into lust, but the desire for these other things – what is it? Curiosity – a desire to apprehend the world in all its rich variety? If so, we should admit that there is great pleasure in curiosity met, in seeing the biggest, smallest and most anything, and that this pleasure drives the world nearly as much as does the desire for beauty. And is not curiosity a more cerebral pleasure, for who imagines embracing the hermaphrodite, eating the giant produce? Is not a hunger for the complexity and variety of the world satisfied, even sated at the State Fair and the sideshow, by seeing? There's a kind of outlaw's exuberance in seeing nature break the rules of decorum and in breaking the rules of good taste oneself; curiosity wants a world whose richness is disorderly and subdued, a desire akin to the infant pleasure of messes and the adolescent pleasure of high-decibel cacophony.

The United States, as Brayton and Barnum and Chesty Morgan (who had her breasts surgically enlarged to the size of, more or less, prize pumpkins) and a thousand Las Vegas designers all demonstrate, is the true home of this aesthetic. Familiar as part of the freak show, the hotdog stands shaped like hotdogs, the roadside dinosaur statuary, this is the aesthetic that would explain why we not only like to look at really beautiful people but also at really obese, tall or tiny ones. It's a curiosity that seems somehow connected to the botanical garden, which attempted to catalogue the expanse of creation's flora as the sideshow does its human fauna. It suggests not a nature of harmony and continuity, but of extravagant experimentation, endless variety, a never-a-dull-moment nature, a wide-open

Vintage 'Exaggerations' postcard, California. Coll. John Pfahl

Vintage postcard, La Jolla, California. Coll. John Pfahl

nature. And perhaps a democratic one, which brings us back to Americanism.

Democratic because it achieves its effect not through exclusion but through inclusion, and because exuberance itself is generally considered to be a little déclassé. There is a whole language of class in the garden: when they returned to the garden, flowers were redeemed with the tasteful monochromatic schemes of the likes of Gertrude Jekyll. As gardening essayist Michael Pollan points out, there is a whole class war of the roses, in which old roses, more fragrant, more softly shaped, less abundant in their bloom, more limited in their palette, are the exiled aristocracy.[12] Good taste is about renunciation: you must have enough to restrain to value restraint, abundance to prize austerity. After all it was only after aniline dyes made bright clothing universally available that the privileged stopped dressing like peacocks, and spareness is often the public face of excess. For those for whom too much is still a shining promise, brightness, quantity, size are not yet dubious qualities. And good taste could also be an aestheticization of the limited-palette moderation of the temperate zone, in contrast to the vividness of the tropics and the starkly sculptural stand-alone forms of desert plants and the desert's period wild bloomings. Moderation, the Greek philosopher said, is pleasant to the wise, but it's not necessarily fun. Eleanor Perenyi writes in her book *Green Thoughts: A Writer in the Garden*:

> Looking at my dahlias one summer day, a friend whose taste runs to the small and impeccable said sadly, 'You do like big, conspicuous flowers, don't you?' She meant vulgar, and I am used to that. It hasn't escaped me that mine is the only WASP garden in town to contain dahlias, and not the discreet little singles either. Some are as blowsy as half-dressed Renoir girls; others are like spiky sea-creatures, water-lilies, or the spirals in a crystal paperweight; and they do shoot up to prodigious heights. But to me they are sumptuous, not vulgar. . . .[13]

Exclusion seeks harmony, familiarity, tranquility, all those things that might be essential to a landscape garden and inimical to a circus – but why can't a garden be like a circus and yield up a circus's gorgeous pleasures? This is the question raised by John Pfahl's photographs, and what makes the answer unusual is that it is entirely botanical.

Often the eccentric gardeners seeking self-expression leave plants out to make gardens of found objects and accretions. These folk art environments proliferate mostly in the American south but can be found almost everywhere and often speak of religion, particularly the Book of Revelation. They are still gardens but they have somehow left nature behind, perhaps because it requires a more patient manipulation than bottles and planks and old tires, perhaps because we tend to think of nature in general as restrained and subdued despite examples of nature in particular like Polonyi's dahlias and Brayton's giraffe, or yuccas whose spray of long leaves looks like fireworks in slow motion. There are other versions of nature that are vibrant, extravagant, even lurid and sensational, and though the most common approximation of Paradise emphasizes its serenity, is not its variety and abundance equally essential? And does not the Book of Revelation with all its architecture of jewels and uncanny beasts suggest that the landscape of revelation is going to be more like the Las Vegas Strip in its neon glory days than, say, the Lake District or the Roman campagna? Was not a long allée of tall trees always secretly offering the pleasures that a row of Vegas showgirls, each six feet tall, now proffers? In which case, plants best approach the ideal nature when the horticulture becomes extreme, an Eden of weirdness and democracy and large appetite for dazzle.

Vintage postcard, Florida. Coll. John Pfahl

notes

1. Henry David Thoreau, from the 'Bean Field' chapter of *Walden,* from *Walden and Other Writings of Henry David Thoreau* (New York: The Modern Library, 1937), p. 140

2. A. J. Dezallier D'Argenville, 'Theory and Practice of Gardening' translated by John James, 1712, in John Dixon Hunt and Peter Willis, *The Genius of the Place: The English Landscape Garden 1620–1820* (Cambridge, MA: The MIT Press, 1988), p. 125

3. Alexander Pope, from a 1713 essay in *The Guardian,* quoted in *The Genius of the Place*, p. 205

4. *ibid.*, p. 208

5. Robert Irwin with Ed Wortz and James Turrell in Lawrence Weschler's *Seeing Is Forgetting the Name of the Thing One Sees: A Life of Contemporary Artist Robert Irwin* (Berkeley: University of California Press, 1982), p. 128. Irwin designed the very peculiar garden at the J. Paul Getty Museum in Los Angeles, a garden that is a sort of sunken basin in whose centre is an inaccessible hedge maze, since it is surrounded by water. The plantings are abundant, and the decision to eliminate the commanding view of the site with descent into the wildly varied floral plantings could be construed as pointed rejection of the monumentally ambitious architecture and commanding location on a high hill.

6. Christopher Thacker *The History of Gardens* (Berkeley: University of California Press, 1979), p. 239

7. John Prest *The Garden of Eden: The Botanic Garden and the Re-Creation of Paradise* (New Haven, CN: Yale University Press, 1981), p. 39

8. *The History of Gardens*, p. 236

9. For example, read Tamar Kahn in the *Johannesburg Business Day* of March 22, 2002: 'For thousands of years the San have used the Hoodia cactus as an appetite suppressant and thirst quencher. It helped them endure long hunts, and resist the temptation to eat their kill before they returned to their camps. The cactus is potentially worth a fortune, because it could very well be the first plant to give rise to a commercially viable appetite suppressant drug. In the US alone, with an estimated 35-million to 65-million clinically obese people, the market for such a product is huge and growing all the time. The central issue in the tale of the cactus, the San, and the international drug companies, is what benefits will the San derive from all of this? That question made international headlines last year, when a British journalist revealed that the Council for Scientific and Industrial Research (CSIR) had patented Hoodia's appetite-suppressing ingredient, dubbed P57, and granted the development rights to Phytopharm, a small pharmaceutical firm in the UK.'

10. John Wesley Powell *The Exploration of the Colorado River and Its Canyons* (New York: Dover Reprint, 1961), p. 22. On the other hand, consider historian Patricia Nelson Limerick on her first trip out of the arid west she was born in: 'As I drove across Oklahoma, crossing what I later learned was the ninety-eighth meridian, discovery joined up with its usual partner, disorientation. The air became humid, clammy, and unpleasant, and the landscape turned distressingly green. The Eastern United States, I learned with every mile, was badly infested with plants. Even where they had been driven back, the bushes, shrubs, and trees gave every sign of anticipating a reconquest. But the even more remarkable fact was this: millions of people lived in this muggy, congested world . . . and considered it normal.' 'Disorientation and Reorientation' from *Something in the Soil: Legacies and Reckonings in the New West* (New York: W. W. Norton, 2000), p. 196

11. Laura Ingalls Wilder, from a digressive portion of her many-volume fictionalized memoirs of growing up on the American frontier, *Farmer Boy*. This book deals with her husband's childhood on a big New York State farm, during which he raises a prize pumpkin and worries about having cheated by making it milk-fed (and the book, as I recall thirty years later, gives details of how he fed this early Miracle-Grow formula to the vine). It must be said, however, that at the Findhorn spiritual community in Scotland in the 1970s, overgrown vegetables became an even more explicit sign of the approval of the gods than did all those county-fair pumpkins and postcards of freightcars bearing a single peach of America the Promised Land.

12. Michael Pollan, *Second Nature: A Gardener's Education* (New York: Random House, 1991), p. 84: 'The war of the roses is at bottom a class war. The tracts of old-rosarians bristle with the fine distinctions, winks, and code words by which aristocrats have always recognized one another.'

13. Eleanor Perenyi, *Green Thoughts: A Writer in the Garden* (New York: Random House, 1981), p. 46–7

Late afternoon sunshine ignites a golden tunnel of grey birches (*Betula populifolia*) at Stan Hywet Gardens near Akron, Ohio. Rubber tycoon and anglophile Franklin A. Seiberling named his extensive estate after a sandstone quarry that was discovered on the property (*stan hywet* means 'stone quarry' in Old English). The 150m/500ft birch allée leads from an imposing 1915 Tudor-style mansion to a panoramic vista over the Cuyahoga River valley.

Birch Allée, Stan Hywet Gardens, Akron, Ohio

Right: Psychiatrist John Wadsworth ruthlessly trimmed this solitary sugar maple (*Acer saccharinum*) to save it from an advanced case of maple die-back disease. It now thrives as a singular work of art, marking the seasons with dramatic changes in colour. Wadsworth, who acts on his creative impulses with a chainsaw, has sculpted numerous other works on his hilltop estate, including mazes, vista allées, and a two-dimensional pine tree.

Left: The same one-armed maple as it appeared a few weeks earlier.

Dr Wadsworth's Tree, Chautauqua, New York

Sunflower Field, Bowmansville, New York

Backyard Pumpkin, Buffalo, New York

Page 22: Weary motorists heading west on the New York State Thruway can catch a welcome glimpse of mammoth Russian sunflowers (*Helianthus annuus*) greeting the sun. The field appears every summer, courtesy of a retired quarry worker who has made it his hobby project. At harvest time, he sells the seeded heads as bird food from a wooden roadside stand, setting out an empty mayonnaise jar to collect payment.

Page 23: Artist Peter Stephens puzzled over a mysterious vine that grew out of his backyard compost pile until it began to set fruit. Then he remembered the Hallowe'en pumpkin he had thrown out the previous fall. When the new pumpkin started to gain weight, Stephens coddled it in a makeshift cradle to protect it from a disastrous plunge.

Right: A showstopper on Buffalo's summer Garden Walk, a sixteen-year-old trumpet vine (*Campsis radicans*) dominates a tiny backyard in the oldest part of town. Dawn Hendryx and Deirdre Baker, the proud caretakers, trim the rampant creeper once a year to pre-empt the telephone company from cutting it down completely.

Backyard Trumpet Vine, Buffalo, New York

In daytime hours throngs of visitors crowd the walkway around the Tidal Basin during Washington DC's annual cherry blossom festival. For a more contemplative communion with the remarkable Yoshino cherry trees, enthusiasts must arrive well before dawn. Many of the trees were originally planted in 1912, part of a shipment of three thousand sent as a gift of friendship to the United States from the people of Japan.

Cherry Trees, Tidal Basin, Washington DC

Cherry Trees, Royal Botanical Gardens, Hamilton, Ontario

Six massive cherry trees (*Prunus* 'Accolade') dominate a gentle rise at the Royal Botanical Gardens arboretum in Hamilton, Ontario. The barrel-shaped trunks are 90cm/3ft in diameter, while each tree's blossoming canopy is some 15m/50ft across. 'Accolade', a relatively new variety, was introduced into Great Britain in 1952 and brought to Canada soon after. It is a cross between *Prunus sargentii* and *P.* x *subhirtella*.

A magical effect is created by midday sunshine filtering through the springtime foliage of this allée of European hornbeams (*Carpinus betulus*). Over 180m/600ft long, it is underplanted with Spanish bluebells (*Hyacinthoides hispanica*), white Siberian squill (*Scilla siberica* 'Alba') and summer snowflakes (*Leucojum aestivum*). It traverses the Niagara Parks Botanical Garden, an outstanding feature of the miles of landscaped parkland along the Niagara River, another being, of course, Niagara Falls.

Hornbeam Vista, Niagara Parks Botanical Garden, Niagara Falls, Ontario

Hedge Demonstration, Royal Botanical Gardens, Hamilton, Ontario

Formal Garden, School of Horticulture, Niagara Falls, Ontario

Page 32: A fantasy of geometric forms, the hedge garden at the Royal Botanical Gardens serves as an educational inspiration for visiting gardeners. Both traditional and uncommon plant materials are shaped into the optimal hedge form: vertical surfaces slant inwards slightly so that the sun can reach lower branches. The following varieties are displayed, from back to front: dwarf burning bush (*Euonymus alatus* `Compactus'), California privet (*Ligustrum ovalifolium*), Thunberg spirea (*Spiraea thunbergii*), European privet (*Ligustrum vulgare*), and Japanese barberry (*Berberis thunbergii*). Also, along the right side, Douglas golden white cedar (*Thuja occidentalis* `Douglasii Aurea').

Page 33: Clearly based on European models, the formal garden in the Niagara Parks Botanical Garden is meticulously groomed by resident students at the associated School of Horticulture. Closely cropped box hedges prevent the late-blooming tulips (*Tulipa* `Maureen' and `Queen of Night') from escaping their beds. In the background, the tall trees of the hornbeam vista (page 30) can be seen.

Right: Rose overload looms at the Hendrie Park Rose Garden, also part of the Royal Botanical Gardens in Hamilton, Ontario. Three varieties of shrub roses, `Prairie Princess', `Bucbi', and `Dornroschen', surround the Kordesii climber `Dortmund'. The RGB, the largest botanical garden in Canada, was established in 1929 and granted a charter by King George V.

Climbing and Shrub Roses, Royal Botanical Gardens, Hamilton, Ontario

Topiary Peacock, Cullen Gardens, Whitby, Ontario

Proudly wearing a crown of *Verbena bonariensis*, an 18m-/60ft-long topiary peacock rests his herbaceous plummage on the lawn of the Cullen Gardens. His 6m-/20ft-high body is covered with 4,600 plants including begonias, coleus, ageratums and *Santolina chamaecyparissus*. Adorning the tail another 6,000 plants include clumps of *Pennisetum*, outlines of *Iresine lindenii*, and accents of *Coleus* 'Tri-color Ducksfoot'. Close to the peacock, jocular topiary hobgoblins chiseled from yew (*Taxus* x *media*) can be found as well (see title page). Part garden, part miniature village, this exuberant 35-acre family attraction near Toronto was opened to the public in 1980.

Busy Rockefeller Center in New York City was the summer 2000 setting for artist Jeff Koons' remarkable 'Puppy'. It was covered with over 70,000 common bedding plants, including petunias, marigolds, impatiens and begonias. Underneath the sculpture's colourful surface, a 13m-/43ft-high stainless steel structure supported twenty-five tons of soil moistened by an elaborate internal irrigation system. 'Puppy' previously appeared in Sydney, Australia and Bilbao, Spain.

Jeff Koons' Puppy, Rockefeller Center, New York

Giraffe Topiary, Green Animals, Portsmouth, Rhode Island

A monumental giraffe fashioned from California privet (*Ligustrum ovalifolium*) surveys the scene at Green Animals overlooking Naragansett Bay. The summer estate was purchased by Thomas Brayton in 1872, and his daughter Alice, with the help of head gardener Joseph Carriero, developed the ever-expanding gardens. The horticultural zoo contains an abundance of whimsical topiary birds and beasts in the shapes of a boar, camel, lion (left), elephant, ostrich, reindeer, swan, two bears and three peacocks, to name just a few.

In the 1940s, Joseph Carriero passed his pruning shears to his son-in-law George Mendonca. For the next fifty years, under his passionate care, Green Animals grew to contain some eighty individual topiaries, including fanciful geometric figures and ornamental designs as well as the twenty-one namesake animals. Mendonca achieved a small amount of fame as one of the stars of Errol Morris' 1997 cult classic film *Fast, Cheap and Out of Control*, which celebrated his gardening prowess.

Geometric Topiary, Green Animals, Portsmouth, Rhode Island

Harvey Smith Ladew, an idiosyncratic New York socialite who died in 1976, was passionate about two things: gardening and fox hunting (which he pursued in the United States and in England). The twin interests are combined in this animated fox hunt scene on the grounds of his estate in the heart of Maryland's hunt country, north of Baltimore. Along with the pack of dogs, a hunter jumps his horse over a fence and the fox scampers away, all expertly sculpted from yew (*Taxus*).

Yew Hunt Scene, Ladew Topiary Gardens, Maryland

The terrace garden at Ladew Topiary Gardens has three levels delineated with Canadian hemlock (*Tsuga canadensis*) hedges and embellished with living obelisks. The fifteen individual gardens on the estate run the gamut from Victorian to rose, berry and water lily. However, visitors are most drawn to the whimsical topiary depicting lyrebirds, unicorns, sea horses, and, most unexpectedly, Winston Churchill's top hat and victory sign.

Hemlock Obelisks, Ladew Topiary Gardens, Maryland

Bare Trees and Topiary, Longwood Gardens, Kennett Square, Pennsylvania

A surreal landscape clipped from Japanese and English yew (*Taxus cuspidata* and *T. baccata*), the topiary compound is a favourite feature at Longwood Gardens. More than fifty specimens grow in twenty different shapes, including cones, cubes, spirals, birds, and a much-loved rabbit. On an early spring day, the gesticulating bare branches of the *Paulownia* trees provide contrast to the verdant topiary.

In the morning sun, espaliered grape vines (*Vitis vinifera* 'Purpurea') and small leaf holly (*Ilex crenata* 'Microphylla') bask against the wall of Longwood Garden's visitors centre. Pierre S. du Pont purchased the estate in 1906 and quickly became passionate about developing the property. There are now eighteen individual gardens, grand allées, extravagant fountains and seven interlocking glass conservatories, one of which (left) is festooned with hanging baskets of marguerite daisies (*Argyranthemum frutescens* 'Vera').

Espalier Demonstration, Longwood Gardens, Kennett Square, Pennsylvania

Longwood's world famous orchid collection boasts many rare and old specimens, as well as the newest hybrids. There are some 9,000 individual plants, representing 3,200 assorted species and cultivars. Scanning the colourful tapestry on the greenhouse wall, one can find pansy orchids (*Miltonia*), the lady's slipper orchid (*Paphiopedilum*), the spider orchid (*Brassia*) and the moth orchid (*Phalaenopsis*). Also of note is the retiring *Epidendrum ilense*, so rare it probably no longer exists in the wild.

Orchid Collection, Longwood Gardens,
Kennett Square, Pennsylvania

Lotus Ponds, Kenilworth Aquatic Gardens, Washington DC

Water Lilies, Kenilworth Aquatic Gardens, Washington DC

Page 54: In mid-July, the lotus blossoms at Kenilworth Aquatic Gardens are at their most exuberant. The show begins at dawn, as thousands of pink and white spherical buds slowly open in concert. The large blossoms, floating above sculptural leaves, summon to mind ancient Egyptian friezes and Japanese screens. The football-field-sized pond was dredged from the tidal marshes of the Anacostia River.

The gardens were started as a hobby in 1880 by Walter B. Shaw, a clerk in the United States Treasury Department, and they became his lifelong passion. When they were threatened with destruction in the 1930s, the government stepped in and created the only American National Park devoted entirely to water-loving plants.

Page 55: Several ponds are devoted solely to tropical water lilies. Especially eye-catching is the extraordinary *Victoria amazonica* from South America, whose platter-like leaves can extend to 1.8 metres/6 feet across. The tubers are stored in greenhouses throughout winter and are moved outdoors in the spring.

Right: Well protected by gates and alarm systems, rare bonsai specimens line up in the airy John Y. Naka North American Pavillion at Washington DC's National Arboretum. From right to left, they are: pasture juniper (*Juniperus communis*), parsley hawthorn (*Crataegus marshallii*), foemina juniper (*Juniperus chinensis* 'Femina'), water elm (*Planera aquatica*) and Scots pine (*Pinus sylvestris*). The National Arboretum has the largest bonsai and penjing collection in the United States, with extraordinary examples from China and Japan, as well as from North America.

Bonsai Collection, National Arboretum, Washington DC

A spectacular cluster of four European weeping beeches (*Fagus sylvatica* 'Pendula') dominates the park at The Elms, one of the premier estates in Newport, Rhode Island. The interior space is cathedral-like in its size, coolness, and subdued light. Designed as an elaborate eighteenth-century French-style château, The Elms was the summer residence of Edward J. Berwind, a Pennyslvania coal magnate. The spacious Classical Revival gardens include a sunken garden, marble pavilions, fountains, and a park of choice specimen trees.

European Weeping Beeches, The Elms, Newport, Rhode Island

Camperdown Elms and Pool, Linwood, New York

Every Camperdown elm (*Ulmus glabra* 'Camperdownii') in the world stems from the mutant Scotch elm found in 1640 on the property of the Earl of Camperdown in Dundee, Scotland. These three healthy specimens, standing alongside their secluded swimming pool, are approaching their first hundred years at Linwood in upstate New York. The estate was created in the early 1900s by William Henry Gratwick II, a Buffalo lumber and shipping magnate. His son, Bill Gratwick III, planted an extensive series of gardens and became renowned as an idiosyncratic artist and hybridizer of tree peonies (left).

Diaphanous threadleaf Japanese maples (*Acer palmatum* var. *dissectum* Dissectum Atropurpureum Group) flaunt their autumn colour not far from the Hershey chocolate factories in the rolling hills of southern Pennsylvania. Approximately 3m/10ft tall and sixty years old, they form part of a large collection of specimen trees generously spaced throughout Hershey Gardens.

Threadleaf Japanese Maples, Hershey Gardens, Pennsylvania

Autumn brings a melancholy atmosphere to the Hershey Rose Garden, following a summer filled with raucous blossoms. First laid out in 1936 by chocolate tycoon Milton Hershey, the hillside garden now contains over 7,000 roses of 275 different varieties, including this delicate arch of *Rosa* 'New Dawn'.

Left: A puppy-like 6m-/20ft-tall weeping Norway spruce (*Picea abies* 'Pendula') looks as if it were about to romp through the grounds on a misty morning.

Autumn Rose Arbor, Hershey Gardens, Pennsylvania

Expanding hourly in warm New England autumn weather, this colossal pumpkin ('Dill's Atlantic Giant') sits regally under a protective canopy. Not long after this photograph was taken, it won first prize for grower Dave Hampton at the Cape Cod Annual Pumpkin Weigh-off. It had matured into the traditional orange pumpkin colour and weighed over 225kg/500lb).

Prize Pumpkin, Cape Cod, Massachusetts

Mums by Paschke, North East, Pennsylvania

The temperate climate near the shores of Lake Erie provides a long growing season for 60,000 chrysanthemums on the 'Mums by Paschke' family farm. Over 150 varieties grown from rooted cuttings are sold at the rustic roadside farm store in North East, Pennsylvania and shipped throughout the eastern half of the United States.

The renowned 'Blue Steps' of Naumkeag, outlined by graceful steel railings and low *Taxus* hedges, descend through a carefully contrived thicket of paper birches (*Betula papyrifera*). Established in the 1880s by New York attorney Joseph Hodges Choate, the estate boasts an elegant shingle-style mansion designed by Sanford White. Choate's daughter Mabel took a passionate interest in the design of the gardens and commissioned well-known landscape architect Fletcher Steel to create a number of distinctive areas. The collaboration culminated in the 'Blue Steps', constructed in 1938. Originally meant as a purely functional way for Miss Choate to get from the house to the cutting garden, it evolved into something much more artful and complex, becoming, in the process, one of the great classics of American garden design.

Paper Birches, Naumkeag, Stockbridge, Massachusetts

Italian Gardens, Sonnenberg Estate, Canandaigua, New York

Scroll Garden, Tryon Palace, New Bern, North Carolina

Page 72: The four sunken parterres of the 'Italian Garden' at Sonnenberg Gardens display decidedly French design influences. Like a flamboyant coat-of-arms, the floral patterns are embroidered with *Solenostemon* 'Red Velvet' 'Goldie', dusty miller (*Senecio cineraria* 'Silver Dust') and Joseph's coat (*Alternanthera ficoidea*). The large estate in Canandaigua, New York, with its eleven unique theme gardens, was created between 1902 and 1923 by Mary Clark Thompson, the widow of a prominent New York banker.

Page 73: An eighteenth-century scroll garden with curving hedges of dwarf yaupon (*Ilex vomitorea*) was imaginatively recreated and planted with ivory Floradale tulips (*Tulipa* 'Maureen') and white pansies (*Viola* 'Crystal Bowl') in New Bern, North Carolina. It can be found on the grounds of the painstakingly restored Tryon Palace, originally built in the early 1770s as a residence for the royal governor when North Carolina was still a British colony. The extensive use of red brick for the convoluted pathways indicates that the garden, even with its heavy European influence, is clearly in the New World.

Right: The sunken garden gracing the Elizabethan Gardens on North Carolina's Roanoke Island is just part of a poetic evocation of a sixteenth-century English pleasure garden. On the site where Sir Walter Raleigh hoped to colonize the New World and where Virginia Dare was born, the first child of English parents in America, the garden was created as a memorial to that ill-fated 'lost' colony. Geometric boxwood parterres inlaid with white, yellow and blue pansies are guarded by twisted early spring crape myrtle standards. They surround the priceless fifteenth-century Italian fountain, pool and balustrade donated by the Honorable John Hay Whitney, ambassador to the Court of St James in the 1950s.

Elizabethan Gardens, Roanoke Island, North Carolina

If this evocative plantation scene looks familiar there may be a reason for it. The oak avenue leading to Boone Hall, near Charleston, South Carolina, is frequently used as a Hollywood location and has featured in numerous movies and television programs. One of the oldest working plantations in the South, Boone Hall was established in 1681 by Major John Boone, a member of the first group of English settlers to arrive in South Carolina. Many of the massive moss-draped oaks were planted by his son, Captain Thomas Boone.

Oaks and Spanish Moss, Boone Hall Plantation, Charleston, South Carolina

ENTER

Maze, Magnolia Plantation, Charleston, South Carolina

The maze at Magnolia Plantation offers a unique American translation of an English prototype. Based on the maze at Hampton Court designed by Henry VIII, it jettisons the original boxwood for five hundred Camellias (*Camellia sasanqua*) interspersed with holly. For three hundred years, Magnolia Plantation has belonged to the American branch of the Drayton family, members of which trace their lineage back to the Norman Conquest and whose ancestral home, Drayton House, is in Northampton, England. A series of romantic southern gardens was reclaimed from swampland (left), mixing cypress trees, azaleas and camellias with lurking alligators and great blue herons.

Resplendent azaleas bloom in early April at the Orton Plantation in North Carolina, thriving in the shade of ancient live oak trees. Once a prosperous antebellum rice plantation, it is now a dreamscape of quintessential Southern plant specialties: camellias, magnolias, oleander, rhododendrons and azaleas. Here, the early-blooming coral bell azaleas (Kurume hybrids) crowd the pathway from the mansion to the lagoon.

Azalea Garden, Orton Hall, Wilmington, North Carolina

This massive banyan tree grew from a tiny sprig in a 19-litre/ 5-gallon can planted at Florida's Cypress Gardens in 1937. A tropical Indian fig tree (*Ficus benghalensis*), it spread quickly and widely by sending down aerial roots from horizontal branches. The roots thickened and formed a network of forest-like trunks, which served to prop up the ever-spreading canopy. To prevent it from overwhelming the rest of the park's extensive botanical garden, it must be trimmed back yearly. Cypress Gardens contains one of the world's largest collections of tropical and sub-tropical plants, amounting to 8,000 varieties from ninety different countries.

Banyan Tree, Cypress Gardens, Florida

Sunday Painter Topiary, Cypress Gardens, Florida

On the shores of Lake Eloise, Cypress Gardens was designed as a series of continuously unfolding pictorial compositions. In fact, Dick Pope Sr, the real estate entrepreneur and publicity genius who, during the Great Depression, wrested this tropical fantasy from the muck of swampland, walked around with a camera's viewfinder while designing the landscape. Here, a topiary 'Southern Belle', styled from sphagnum moss and English ivy (*Hedera helix*), sketches some of the numerous cypress trees that give the gardens their name.

Mother Bird and Young, Cypress Gardens, Florida

Fifty-foot Inchworm, Cypress Gardens, Florida

Pages 86–7 and right: The grandfather of Florida's tourist industry, Cypress Gardens lay the groundwork for today's modern theme parks, including Disney World and Busch Gardens. 'If it ain't fun, then the heck with it!' – Dick Pope's motto is borne out annually at the Spring Flower Festival. Twenty-four topiary animals are whimsically scattered among floral beds containing 30,000 bedding plants. Standouts among the botanical birds, beasts, and butterflies are a gigantic cardinal feeding her babies, a 15m-/50ft-long inchworm, and a brilliantly coloured tropical fish.

Designed by chief horticulturist Joe Freeman, the topiaries represent long months of planning and construction. Working from miniature clay models, the park's maintenance engineers welded more than 26km/17 miles of steel to fabricate the sculptural frameworks. 14,500kg/15 tons of the growing medium, sphagnum moss, was applied to the outer layers, then hand-planted with 34,000 impatiens and begonias. Internal timer-controlled sprinkling systems supply water and liquid fertilizer during the two-month long display.

Begonia Fish, Cypress Gardens, Florida

An elegant great white egret poses on one of the 'Famous Floating Islands' in a lagoon at Epcot. The playful display of intensely coloured impatiens (*Impatiens walleriana*) on some two hundred floating islands is part of the Epcot International Flower and Garden Festival held annually at Walt Disney World Resort. Featured at the six-week event are 1,200 plant species from around the world embellishing the 300-acre park with millions of flowers.

Impatiens Islands with Egret, Epcot, Walt Disney World Resort, near Orlando, Florida
(Used by permission from Disney Enterprises, Inc.)

A luminous grove of smooth-trunked Bailey palms (*Copernicia baileyana*) represents only a small fraction of the extensive palm collection at Fairchild Tropical Gardens near Miami. Over 500 species of palms – including (left) the gebang palm (*Corypha utan*) with its gigantic fronds – surround numerous alligator-friendly ponds and lakes. Named after David Fairchild, a botanist and plant explorer who collected many of the original specimens in the 1940s, the garden is one of the largest of its kind in the world and promotes botanical research and conservation of rare species.

Palm Walk, Fairchild Tropical Gardens, Coral Gables, Florida

A vision of pristine Southwest desert appears at a busy intersection near downtown Tucson, Arizona. Liberal use was made of indigenous desert plants such as the giant saguaro (*Carnegiea gigantea*), ocotillo (*Fouquieria splendens*), and desert spoon (*Dasylirion wheeleri*), making the ultimate in low-maintenance gardens. The photograph was taken close to the time of its original planting, but it has evolved over the years into a greener, far less barren, landscape. The project was designed by landscape architect John Hucko for the Acacia Group.

Highway Cactus Planting, Tucson, Arizona

Right: A striking tableau greets visitors to the Huntington Desert Garden in San Marino, California. Home of one of the most important collections of cacti and succulents in the world, this living botanical reference library contains over a thousand different species. In the dense grouping, the following plants can be found: night blooming cereus (*Hylocereus undatus*), giant saguaro (*Carnegiea gigantea*), golden barrel cactus (*Echinocactus grusonii*) bunny ears (*Opuntia microdasys*) and blue kleinia (*Senecio repens*).

Left above: Creeping devil (*Stenocereus eruca*).

Left below: Variegated century plant (*Agave americana* 'Variegata').

Huntington Desert Garden South Entrance, San Marino, California

Eighty-year old golden barrel cacti (*Echinocactus grusonii*) march towards the fading light under bottle palms (*Nolina recurvata*) and *Trichocereus pasacana* at the Huntington Desert Garden. The site of the Huntington Library, Art Collections and Botanical Gardens was originally the ranch and winter home of Henry E. Huntington, wealthy owner of two California railroads. In fact, many of the plant materials and rocks from across the country and from Mexico were transported directly to his gardens by Huntington's own freight cars.

Golden Barrel Cacti, Huntington Desert Garden, San Marino, California

Tim Curry's Garden, East View, Hollywood, California

Tim Curry's Garden, North View, Hollywood, California

Prickly Pear Cacti, Fullerton Arboretum, Fullerton, California

Page 100–101: When British stage and film actor Tim Curry bought a secluded hacienda in the Hollywood Hills near Griffith Park, he immediately set about cleaning up the yard. What he discovered to his great delight, after removing some forty tons of accumulated debris, was the long-buried skeleton of an original 1920s garden designed by architect Stiles O. Clements. Together with landscape designer Barry Sattels, Curry rescued a network of stone paths, pools and watercourses in what amounted to an extensive archaeological dig. They planted an impressive collection of palms, cacti, and succulents that clamber up near-vertical terrain of the two-acre amphitheater-like space. The densely textured tapestry includes numerous varieties of aloes and agaves, the spiky desert spoon (*Dasylirion wheeleri*), the brilliant sticks on fire (*Euphorbia tirucalli*), coral aloe (*Aloe striata*), golden barrel cacti (*Echinocactus grusonii*) and *Trichocereus* cacti.

Left: Lacking the long nasty spines of other prickly pear cacti, bunny ears (*Opuntia microdasys*), like their namesake, seem to invite caressing fingers. Not a good idea, since their padded surfaces are covered with a multitude of tiny barbed spines called glochids that easily stick in the skin in a most irritating manner. This ever-expanding congregation can be found at the Fullerton Arboretum, a large botanical garden on the campus of the California State University in Fullerton.

Choosing plants that would thrive on the dry and windy south promontory of the Getty Center, landscape architects Laurie Olin and Dennis McGlade created a startling composition that visitors can only see from above. Variegated century plants (*Agave americana* 'Variegata'), golden barrel cacti (*Echinocactus grusonii*), and the pincer-like psychoactive San Pedro cacti (*Trichocereus pachanoi*) combine to form a city in miniature that cleverly puns on the city of Los Angeles in the hazy distance. Critics have likened the unapproachable terrace to a rest stop for aliens from outer space, or, more mundanely, to a wholesale cactus nursery.

Cactus Garden, J. Paul Getty Center,
Los Angeles, California

A focal point of artist Robert Irwin's extravagant commissioned garden, the azalea maze seems to float on the surface of a watery reflecting pool. At once cerebral and sensuous, the garden, with its abundant plantings and meandering stream, offers a cool, midday refuge from architect Richard Meier's shimmering travertine edifice higher up (left).

Azalea Maze, J. Paul Getty Center, Los Angeles, California

The eccentric branching of the relaxed euphoria (*Euphorbia ingens*) seems to reflect the colourful personality of the late Ganna Walska, who purchased the estate she later called 'Lotusland' in 1941. Married six times, this former Polish opera singer had a passion for millionaire husbands, Tibetan mysticism, and extravagant gardening. She bought cacti and euphorbia by the lorryload to landscape her 1920s Mediterranean-style mansion.

Relaxed Euphorbia, Lotusland, Montecito, California

Lotusland's thirty-seven acres contain numerous sub-gardens devoted to specific plants or concepts. The cycad garden, with its world-class collection of primordial plants, the idiosyncratic aloe garden decorated with giant abalone shells and the lotus-filled water garden provide surprises at every turn.

A sociable group of *Agave franzosinii* and *Furcraea roezlii* guard the bromeliad section (right). In the ethereal blue garden (left, above), Mexican fan palms parade on a carpet of blue chalk sticks (*Senecio mandraliscae*) and blue fescue (*Festuca glauca*). And, in the Japanese garden (left, below) the unusual Costa Rican weeping bamboo (*Chusquea coronalis*) hangs its lachrymose canes over a small sea of baby's tears (*Soleirolia soleirolii*).

Agave Collection, Lotusland, Montecito, California

Australian brush cherry topiaries (*Syzygium paniculatum*) flank the path to Lotusland's swimming pool in the fern garden. Oversized Australian tree ferns (*Sphaeropteris cooperi*) can reach 4.5m/15ft in height. In her later years (she lived to ninety-seven years), Madame Walska was frequently to be seen walking slowly along the paths of her beloved retreat.

Fern Garden, Lotusland, Montecito, California

The Largest Fig Tree in the United States, Santa Barbara, California

Left: A seedling imported by a visiting sailor in 1876 has grown into the largest Moreton Bay fig tree (*Ficus macrophylla*) in North America. Twice as wide as it is tall, it spreads its magnificent crown over 53m/175ft. The City of Santa Barbara designated it as an official historic landmark in 1970.

Page 116: Sprawling 'McMansions', as they are sometimes called, sprout like mushrooms on the hills above Pismo Beach, taking advantage of spectacular ocean views. Here, newly planted azaleas and other groundcover plants embroider a king-sized burlap carpet laid down to preserve moisture and prevent erosion. Pismo Beach, a classic old California resort town, half way between Los Angeles and San Francisco, is known for clams, whales and migrating Monarch butterflies.

Page 117: Sculpted *Podocarpus macrophyllus* cubes and magnolias flank a long reflecting pool mirroring a pyramidal fountain and a glass-covered skyscraper in downtown Los Angeles. It is a small component of the ambitious two-billion-dollar California Plaza redevelopment project that encompasses office buildings, a luxury hotel and the Museum of Contemporary Art, along with pedestrian-friendly plazas and fountains. The contemplative sanctuary in the midst of urban chaos was designed by landscape architect Joe Yee.

Burlap Garden in New Subdivision, Pismo Beach, California

Podocarpus Cubes, California Plaza, Los Angeles, California

A frieze of Hollywood junipers (*Juniperus chinensis* 'Torulosa') intermingled with bougainvillea gives visual evidence of prevailing ocean breezes. The contrasting vegetation borders the entrance to an upscale mobile-home park on a bluff overlooking the Pacific in Palos Verdes, California. The 'Age 55 and Better Community' advertises a nine-hole golf course, floodlit tennis courts, shuffleboard, and a heated swimming pool, all access-protected by a 24-hour gatehouse. Not far away (left) a rampant bougainvillea borders a public parking area.

Junipers and Bougainvillea, Palos Verdes, California

On the first French voyage of exploration to the Pacific Ocean, a spectacularly colourful vine was found in Brazil by naturalist Philibert Commerson. He named it after the captain of the ship, Louis Antoine de Bougainville. Today, found espaliered against a long wall near fashionable Los Feliz Boulevard, Bougainvillea 'Barbara Karst' and 'Brasiliensis' provide a visual treat for passing motorists. The vibrant colours do not come from the diminutive flowers of this vine, but from the large paper-like bracts that surround them.

Wall with *Bougainvillea*, Los Feliz, California

Fashion Island Palm Trees, Newport Beach, California

Las Vegas Strip Beautification Project, Las Vegas, Nevada

Ice Plant Interchange, Carlsbad, California

Page 122: When the sun sets in parts of California and Nevada, decorative plants light up the night. The tallest of these are Canary Island date palms (*Phoenix canariensis*), often lined up like chorus girls, as at the grand entrance to Fashion Island, a mega-mall shopping complex in Newport Beach, California.

Page 123: A profusion of palms lines the centre median of Las Vegas Boulevard in front of the black pyramid of the Luxor Hotel and Casino. Included are the ubiquitous Canary Island date palms, windmill palms (*Trachycarpus fortunei*), and *Butia* x *Syagrus* hybrid palms. The thirteen-million-dollar Las Vegas Strip beautification project, in which 76,000 palms and shrubs are deployed, was completed in 1996. A ten-storey replica of the Sphinx guards the Egyptian-theme hotel and its version of King Tut's tomb.

Left: Most highway interchanges in California are quite unremarkable, but the cartoon-like colors at an Interstate 5 exit near Carlsbad dazzle the eye. Fluorescent rosea ice plants (*Drosanthemum floribundum*) jostle patches of red-orange ivy geraniums (*Pelargonium peltatum*) forming a brilliant carpet under a colonnade of lemon-scented gum trees (*Eucalyptus citriodora*). The imaginative plantings were designed by Caltrans landscape architect Heidi P. Martin and are carefully maintained by nearby Legoland theme park.

Native to Asia Minor, *Ranunculus asiaticus* (left) is a member of the buttercup family and is commonly referred to as the Persian buttercup. In the 1920s botanist Luther Gage brought back some of the exotic seeds from England and found that the plants flourished in the mild winters and dry summers of the California coast near San Diego. The result, with constant innovative hybridizing over the years, is the Flower Fields, a spreading commercial venture that is a working ranch, garden centre and tourist attraction all in one, welcoming more than 150,000 visitors each year.

The Flower Fields, Carlsbad, California

As if powered by nearby high-tension wires, this profuse display of white Lady Banks roses (*Rosa banksiae*), native to China, threatens to explode with blossoms. The International Rosarium at Descanso Gardens was laid out in the late 1940s by eminent rose breeder Walter Lammerts and renovated in 1994. The five-acre garden has more than 4,000 roses harmoniously interspersed with companion plantings of perennials and shrubs. The original Rancho del Descanso was created by newspaper publisher Manchester Boddy in 1937 and is famous for its magnificent camellia forest.

Lady Banks Rose Arbor, Descanso Gardens,
La Cañada, California

Largest Wisteria in the United States, Sierra Madre, California

Can one really believe the inscription emblazoned on this plaque near a monstrous wisteria vine in a comfortable Sierra Madre backyard?

WORLD'S LARGEST BLOOMING PLANT

THIS WORLD FAMOUS WISTARIA (*sic*) VINE, ONE OF THE 7 HORTICULTURAL WONDERS OF THE WORLD, WAS PLANTED IN 1894 FROM A ONE GALLON POT. LISTED AS 'WORLD'S LARGEST BLOSSOMING PLANT' BY THE GUINESS BOOK OF WORLD RECORDS, IT COVERS NEARLY ONE ACRE AND HAS OVER 1,500,000 BLOSSOMS DURING ITS FIVE WEEK BLOOMING PERIOD.

Roozengaarde, a fanciful display garden for tulips and other springtime flowers, is one of the great draws for visitors to the annual Skagit Valley Tulip Festival. Here, a cloud-formed juniper floats above a composition of tulips (Tulipa 'Red Appledoorn', 'Yellow Appledoorn' and 'Angelique') and daffodils (Narcissus 'Red Hill' and 'Geranium'). Enclosing the garden is a row of pussy willows (Salix discolor); their tops cut off to keep growth in check.

Roozengaarde Display Garden, Skagit Valley, Washington

An inland sea of scarlet tulips (*Tulipa* 'Ile de France') covers 30 acres of sandy soil in the Skagit Valley near the Puget Sound. Dutch settlers started coming here in the 1930s after the federal government placed an embargo on bulb imports. William and Helen Roozen arrived from Holland in 1947 to start a family and continue their ancestral bulb-growing traditions. Their efforts eventually evolved into the family-owned Washington Bulb Company and into a total of thirty-five grandchildren.

Washington Bulb Company Tulip Field,
Skagit Valley, Washington

Poplar-Cottonwood Hybrid Tree Farm, Skagit Valley, Washington

Cloning has been developed into a high art form in the hybrid poplar-cottonwood plantations that are a multi-million-dollar industry in the Pacific Northwest. In a practice more like agriculture than forestry, these fast growing trees can be harvested in as little as six years after planting having reached an average height of more than 18m/60ft. Approximately 45,000 acres are currently in production in Washington and Oregon, supplying pulp for the manufacture of various paper products.

Filoli, a dramatic estate developed in the early 1900s by gold mining magnate William Bowers Bourne II inhabits an unusually felicitous microclimate in the hills south of San Francisco. Two hundred yews, started from small cuttings brought over from Ireland, punctuate its many gardens. Visitors can stroll along the stately yew allée to the High Place, where they are treated to an expansive view of the gardens, house and fields beyond. A miniature knot garden (left), no larger than a card table, can be found surrounded by a more conventionally scaled knot garden.

Yew Allée, Filoli Gardens, Woodside, California

gardens open to the public

The following gardens and arboretums are open to the public. Information on hours, admission prices, tours, and driving directions can be obtained by writing, calling or visiting web sites.

BOONE HALL PLANTATION
Post Office Box 1554
Mount Pleasant, South Carolina
29465

(843) 884-4371
www.boonehallplantation.com

CULLEN GARDENS
300 Taunton Road, West
Whitby, Ontario
L1N 5R5 Canada

(905) 668-6606
www.cullengardens.com

CYPRESS GARDENS
Post Office Box 1
Cypress Gardens, Florida
33884-0009

(800) 282-2133
(863) 324-2111
www.cypressgardens.com

DESCANSO GARDENS
1418 Descanso Drive
La Canada, California
91011-3102

(818) 952-4400
www.descanso.com

THE ELMS
Newport, Rhode Island
  Mailing Address:
The Preservation Society of Newport County
424 Bellevue Avenue
Newport, Rhode Island
02840-6924

(401) 847-1000
www.newportmansions.org

ELIZABETHAN GARDENS
Elizabethan Garden Club of North Carolina, Inc.
Post Office Box 1150
Manteo, North Carolina
27954

(252) 473-3234
www.outerbanks.com/elizabethangardens

FAIRCHILD TROPICAL GARDEN
10901 Old Cutler Road
Coral Gables, Florida
33156-4233

(305) 667-1651
www.ftg.org

FILOLI CENTER
86 Canada Road
Woodside, California
94062-4144

(650) 366-7836
www.filoli.org

THE FLOWER FIELDS
5704 Paseo Del Norte
Carlsbad, California
92008-4435

(760) 431-0352
www.theflowerfields.com

FULLERTON ARBORETUM
1900 Associated Road
at Yorba Linda Boulevard
Fullerton, California
92831-1659

(714) 278-3579
www.arboretum.fullerton.edu

THE J. PAUL GETTY MUSEUM
Visitor Services
1200 Getty Center Drive, Suite 1000
Los Angeles, California
90049-1687

(310) 440-7305
www.getty.edu

GREEN ANIMALS
Portsmouth, Rhode Island
  Mailing address:
The Preservation Society of Newport County
424 Bellevue Avenue
Newport, Rhode Island
02840-6924

(401) 847-1000
www.newportmansions.org/connoisseurs/greenanimals.html

HERSHEY GARDENS
170 Hotel Road
Hershey. Pennsylvania
17033-9507

(717) 534-3492
www.hersheygardens.com

THE HUNTINGTON LIBRARY, ART COLLECTIONS, AND BOTANICAL GARDENS
1151 Oxford Road
San Marino, California
91108-1218

(626) 405-2140
www.huntington.org

KENILWORTH PARK AND AQUATIC GARDENS
National Park Service
1900 Anacostia Drive, SE
Washington, DC
20020-6722

(202) 426-6905
www.nps.gov/nace/keaq

LADEW TOPIARY GARDENS
3535 Jarrettsville Pike
Monkton, Maryland
2111-1910

(301) 57-9570
www.ladewgardens.com

LINWOOD
Linwood, New York

(585) 584-3229

LONGWOOD GARDENS
Post Office Box 501
Kennett Square, Pennsylvania
19348-0501

(610) 388-1000
www.longwoodgardens.org

GANNA WALSKA LOTUSLAND
695 Ashley Road
Santa Barbara, California
93108-1059

(805) 969-3767
www.lotusland.org

MAGNOLIA PLANTATION AND GARDENS
3550 Ashley River Road
Charleston, South Carolina
29414-7109

(800) 367-3517
(843) 571-1266
www.magnoliaplantation.com

MUMS BY PASCHKE
12286 East Main Road
North East, Pennsylvania
16428-3646

(814) 725-9860

UNITED STATES NATIONAL ARBORETUM
3501 New York Avenue, NE
Washington, DC
20002-1958

(202) 245-2726
www.usna.usda.gov

NAUMKEAG
5 Prospect Hill Road
Stockbridge, Massachusetts
01262

(413) 298-3239
www.berkshireweb.com/trustees/naumkeag.html

THE NIAGARA PARKS COMMISSION
School of Horticulture
2565 Niagara Parkway
Post Office Box 150
Niagara Falls, Ontario
L2E 6T2 Canada

(905) 356-8554
www.niagaraparks.com

ORTON PLANTATION GARDENS
9149 Orton Road, SE
Winnabow, North Carolina
28479-5277

(910) 371-6851
www.ortongardens.com

ROOZENGAARDE
Tulips.com
Post Office Box 1248
Mt. Vernon, Washington
98273

(866) 488-5477
www.tulips.com

ROYAL BOTANICAL GARDENS
680 Plains Road, West
Burlington, Ontario
L7T 4H4

(905) 527-1158
www.rbg.ca

SONNENBERG MANSION AND GARDENS
151 Charlotte Street
Canandaigua, New York
14424-1363

(585) 394-4922
www.sonnenberg.org

STAN HYWET HALL AND GARDENS
714 North Portage Path
Akron, Ohio
44303-1399

(330) 836-5533
www.stanhywet.org

TRYON PALACE HISTORIC SITES AND GARDENS
Post Office Box 1007
New Bern, North Carolina
28563-1007

(800) 767-1560
(252) 514-4900
www.tryonpalace.org

plant index

A

Acer
A. palmatum var. dissectum
Dissectum Atropurpureum
Group 62
A. saccharinum 20
Agave
A. americana 'Variegata' 96, 104
A. franzosinii 110
ageratums 38
aloe, coral (A. striata) 103
Alternanthera ficoidea 74
Argyranthemum frutescens 'Vera'
50
azaleas 79, 106, 115
Kurume hybrids 80
coral bell 80

B

baby's tears 110
bamboo, Costa Rican weeping 110
banyan 83
barberry, Japanese 34
beech, European weeping 59
begonias 38, 88
Berberis thunbergii 34
Betula
B. papyrifera 70
B. populifolia 18
birch
grey, 18
paper 70
bluebells, Spanish 30
bougainvillea 118
B. 'Barbara Karst' 121
B. 'Brasiliensis' 121
Brassia 52
bunny ears 96, 103
burning bush, dwarf 34
Butia x Syagrus 125

C

cactus,
golden barrel 96, 98, 103, 104
San Pedro 104
camellia 79, 80
C. sasanqua 79

Campsis radicans 24
Carnegiea gigantea 95, 96
Carpinus betulus 30
cedar, Douglas golden white 34
century plant, variegated 96, 104
cereus, night blooming 96
chalk sticks, blue 110
cherry 27, 29
Australian brush 112
chrysanthemums 69
Chusquea coronalis 110
coleus 38
C. 'Tri-color Ducksfoot' 38
Copernicia baileyana 92
Corypha utan 92
Crataegus marshallii 56
creeping devil 96
cycads 110
cypress 79, 85

D

daffodils 132
daisies, marguerite 50
Dasylirion wheeleri 95, 103
desert spoon 95, 103
Drosanthemum floribundum 125
dusty miller 74

E

Echinocactus grusonii 96, 98, 103,
104
elm
Camperdown 61
water 56
Epidendrum ilense 52
Eucalyptus citrodora 125
Euonymus alatus 'Compactus' 34
euphorbia, relaxed 109
E. tirucalli 103
E. ingens 109

F

Fagus sylvatica 'Pendula' 59
fern, Australian tree 112
fescue, blue
Festuca glauca 110
Ficus

F. benghalensis 83
F. macrophylla 115
fig
Indian 83
Moreton Bay 115
Fouquieria splendens 95
Furcraea roezlii 110

G

geraniums, ivy 125
gum tree 125

H

hawthorn, parsley 56
Hedera helix 85
Helianthus annuus 24
hemlock, Canadian 46
holly 79
small leaf 50
hornbeam 34
European 30
Hyacinthoides hispanica 30
Hylocereus undatus 96

I

Ilex
I. crenata 'Microphylla' 50
I. vomitoria 74
impatiens 38, 88, 91
I. walleriana 91
Irisene lindenii 37
ivy, English 85

J

Joseph's coat 74
juniper
foemina 56
Hollywood 118
pasture 56
Juniperus
J. chinensis 'Torulosa' 118
J.c. 'Femina' 56
J. communis 56

K

kleinia, blue 96

L

Leucojum aestivum 30
Ligustrum
L. ovalifolium 34, 41
L. vulgare 34
lotus 56

M

magnolias 80, 115
maple
sugar 20
threadleaf Japanese 62
marigolds 38
Miltonia 52
myrtle, crape 74

N

Narcissus
N. 'Geranium' 132
N. 'Red Hill' 132
Nolina recurvata 98

O

oak 76, 80
ocotillo 95
oleander 80
Opuntia microdasys 96, 103
orchid
lady's slipper 52
moth 52
pansy 52
spider 52

P

palm
Bailey 92
bottle 98
Canary Island date 125
gebang 92
Mexican fan 110
windmill 125
pansies, 74
Paphiopedilum 52
Paulownia 49
Pelargonium peltatum 125
Pennisetum 38
petunias 38

Phalaenopsis 52
Phoenix canariensis 125
Picea abies 'Pendula' 64
pine, Scots 56
Pinus sylvestris 56
Planera aquatica 56
Podocarpus macrophyllus 115
poplar-cottonwood 137
privet
Californian 34, 41
European 34
Prunus
P. 'Accolade' 29
P. sargentii 29
P. x subhirtella 29
pumpkin
'Dill's Atlantic Giant' 66
Hallowe'en 24
pussy willow 132

R

Ranunculus asiaticus 126
rhododendrons 80
rosea ice plants 125
roses (Rosa) 34, 46, 64
'Bucbi' 34
'Dornroschen' 34
'Dortmund' 34
Lady Banks (R. banksiae) 129
'New Dawn' 64
'Prairie Princess' 34

S

saguaro, giant 95, 96
Salix discolor 132
Santolina chamaecyparissus 38
Scilla siberica 'Alba' 30
Senecio
S. cineraria 'Silver Dust' 74
S. mandraliscae 110
S. repens 96
snowflakes, summer 30
Soleirolia soleirolii 110
Solenostemon 'Red Velvet' 74
Sphaeropteris cooperi 112
Spirea thunbergii 34
spruce, weeping Norway 64

squill, white Siberian 30
Stenocereus eruca 96
sticks on fire 103
sunflower, Russian 24
Syzygium paniculatum 112

T

Taxus 44, 70
T. baccata 49
T. cuspidata 49
Thuja occidentalis 'Douglasii Aurea'
34
Trachycarpus fortunei 125
tree peonies
Trichocereus 103
T. pachanol 104
T. pasacana 98
Tsuga canadensis 46
tulips (Tulipa) 34, 74, 132, 134
'Angelique' 132
'Ile de France' 134
'Maureen' 34, 74
'Queen of the Night' 34
'Red Appledoorn' 132
'Yellow Appledoorn' 132

U

Ulmus glabra 'Camperdownii' 61

V

Verbena bonariensis 38
Victoria amazonica 56
vine
grape 50
trumpet 24
Viola 'Crystal Bowl' 74
Vitis vinifera 'Purpurea' 50

W

water lilies 46, 56
wisteria 131

Y

yaupon, dwarf 74
yew 44, 138
English 49
Japanese 49

Frances Lincoln Limited
4 Torriano Mews
Torriano Avenue
London NW5 2RZ
www.franceslincoln.com

British Library Cataloguing-in-publication data.
A catalogue record for this book is available from the British Library.

ISBN 0 7112 2012 3

Printed and bound in China by Kwong Fat Offset Printing Co. Ltd

9 8 7 6 5 4 3 2 1

FRONTISPIECE
Smiling Topiary, Cullen Gardens, Whitby, Ontario